THE STUDENT BIBLE ATLAS
Revised Edition

Dr Tim Dowley

Contents

Introduction

Although the Bible contains the message of salvation for all peoples in all times, it originates in a particular place and at a particular time. It does not consist of a set of philosophical ideas or academic theories, but tells the story of God's dealings with a particular people – the Jews.

The history of the Jews was bound up with their land: 'The land you are entering to take over is not like the land of Egypt, from which you have come, where you planted your seed and irrigated it by foot as in a vegetable garden. But the land you are crossing the Jordan to take possession of is a land of mountains and valleys that drinks rain from heaven. It is a land that the LORD your God cares for; the eyes of the LORD your God are continually on it from the beginning of the year to its end' (Deuteronomy 11:10–12).

The Bible is full of journeys. We follow Abraham on his epic journey from his father's home in Ur to the land of Canaan. We follow the Hebrews on their journey from slavery in Egypt to their eventual arrival in the Promised Land. We read about the growth of the kingdom of Israel under King David; and later about the exile and return of the people of Judah.

In the New Testament we follow Jesus on his travels around Palestine, and Paul on his unique series of missionary journeys. Finally we trace the letters from John to the Seven Churches of Asia Minor.

But now, centuries later, and in lands distant from Palestine, it is helpful to have maps to show us where all these places were,

The Western Wall, Jerusalem which incorporates masonry dating from the time of Herod the Great.

and where the travelers went. What was Mesopotamia? Where did Moses cross the Red Sea? Why were so many battles fought across the length and breadth of Palestine? Where was Golgotha – the Place of the Skull? And where was it that Paul's merchant ship foundered on the voyage to Rome?

All these questions are answered – or at least illuminated – by the maps in this book. We have not attempted to produce a book for university professors and research students – they have plenty readily available – but a clear, straightforward set of maps that will provide an accessible backdrop to the Bible narrative.

The Atlas also includes a gazetteer. By looking up the place you want to find in the gazetteer, you will find a map number and grid reference for locating it on each map where it appears.

Preface to Revised Edition

The Student Bible Atlas was first published in 1989 and has since been translated into more than twenty-five languages worldwide. For this revised edition every map has been re-created using new digital resources, and every location checked and updated. A completely new selection of photographs has been included, and the gazetteer carefully revised and reviewed. Every effort has been taken to ensure that this tool for biblical research and study is as useful as possible for the twenty-first century reader.

Tim Dowley, May 2015

The western shore of the Dead Sea. Some of the rocks are coated in salt crystals.

APENNINE MOUNTAINS

ADRIATIC SEA

R. Danube

BALKAN MOUNTAINS

MACEDONIA

● Rome

ITALY

GREECE

AEGEAN SEA

● Athens

● Ephesus

CRETE

M E D I T E R R A N E A N   S E A

MAP 1

Lands of the Bible

Palestine – at the cross-roads of the ancient world, fought over countless times across the centuries – lies at the western end of the Fertile Crescent. This great arc of low-lying, well-watered, cultivable land stretches from the Persian Gulf to the Nile Delta. Mesopotamia, 'the land between the rivers', makes up a large part of the Crescent, and was one of the cradles of civilization.

LIBYA

Alexandria ●

LOWER EGY

Memphis
(Noph)

WESTERN DESERT

LIBYAN DESERT

R. Nil

UPPER
EGYPT

Camels in the Syrian Desert.

BLACK SEA

CAUCASUS MOUNTAINS

KARAKUM

ARMENIA

CASPIAN SEA

ASIA

ATOLIAN PLATEAU

RUS MOUNTAINS

CYPRUS

SYRIA

Antioch

SYRIAN DESERT

MESOPOTAMIA

Nineveh

R. Tigris

ZAGROS MOUNTAINS

PERSIA

R. Euphrates

Damascus

PALESTINE

Babylon

Jerusalem

DEAD SEA

Ur

SINAI

PERSIAN GULF

ERN DESERT

RED SEA

hebes

Fertile Crescent

Major ancient highway

0	100	200	300	400	500 km
0		100		200	300 miles

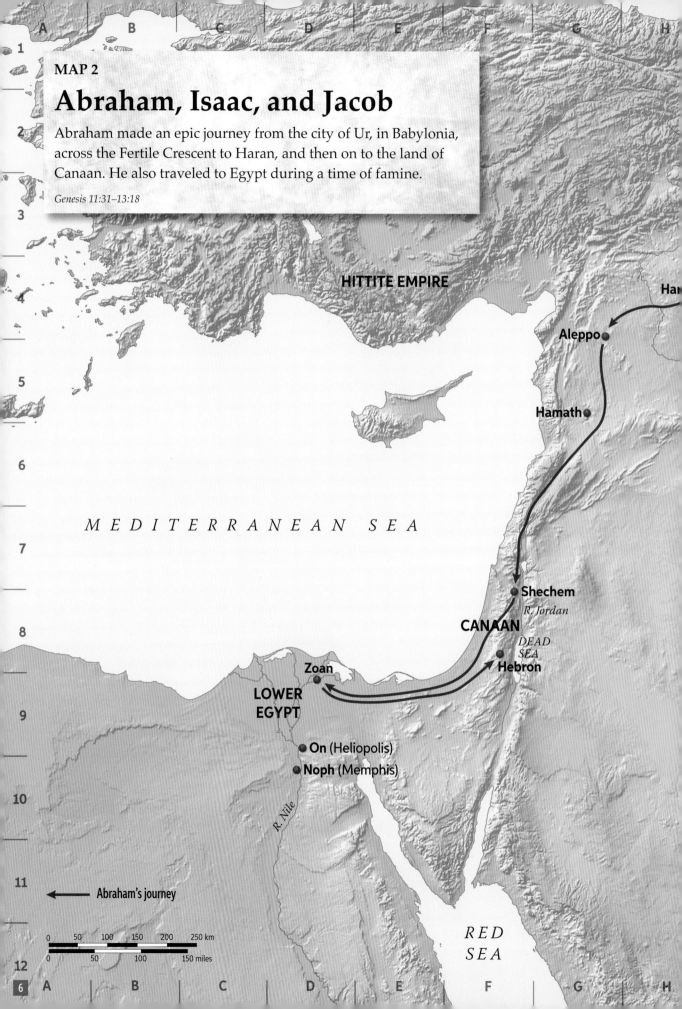

MAP 2

Abraham, Isaac, and Jacob

Abraham made an epic journey from the city of Ur, in Babylonia, across the Fertile Crescent to Haran, and then on to the land of Canaan. He also traveled to Egypt during a time of famine.

Genesis 11:31–13:18

HITTITE EMPIRE

Har

Aleppo

Hamath

MEDITERRANEAN SEA

Shechem

R. Jordan

CANAAN

DEAD SEA

Zoan

Hebron

LOWER EGYPT

On (Heliopolis)

Noph (Memphis)

R. Nile

Abraham's journey

| 0 | 50 | 100 | 150 | 200 | 250 km |
| 0 | | 50 | | 100 | 150 miles |

RED SEA

MAP 3

Abraham's Family in Canaan

Abraham took with him his family, sheep, and goats, to lead a new nomadic life in the hills and plains of his adopted land, Canaan, finally settling near Hebron. His grandson, Jacob, ended his days in Egypt, with his favorite son Joseph.

Genesis 27–46

Artist's impression of a Mesopotamian ziggurat.

MAP 4

The Exodus

Abraham's descendants, the Hebrews, remained in Egypt for some 400 years, becoming enslaved by the Egyptians. Finally, after a series of terrible plagues, Moses led them out of Egypt, across the Red Sea and into the desert. We cannot be sure which route they took; the map shows the traditional route and two alternatives. (They would not have taken the direct, coastal route, since it was guarded.) At Mt Sinai Moses received the Ten Commandments.

Exodus, Numbers

MEDITERRANEAN SEA

NILE DELTA

Rameses (Zoan)

GOSHEN

WILDERNESS OF SHUR

Succoth

Pithom

GREAT BITTER LAKE

EGYPT

On (Heliopolis)

Noph (Memphis)

SINAI PENINSU...

R. Nile

Marah ?

Elim?

The Sphinx, Cairo, Egypt.

← Traditional route

◄······ Alternative routes

◄······ Way to the Land of the Philistines

RED SEA

Mt Sin... (Hore...

| 0 | 20 | 40 | 60 | 80 | 100 km |

| 0 | 20 | 40 | 60 miles |

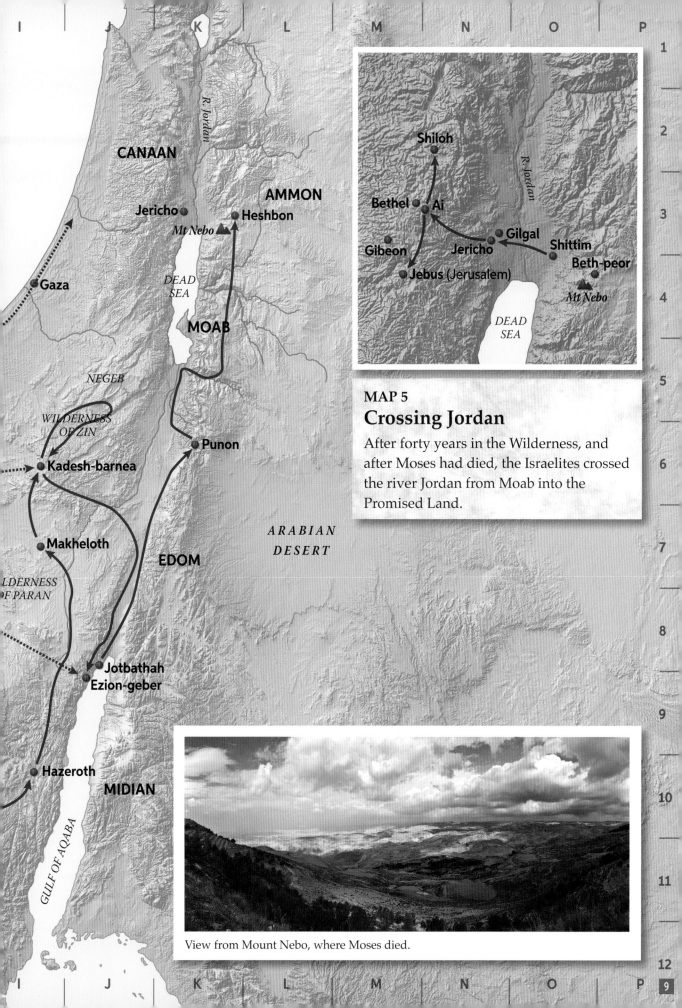

I J K L M N O P

CANAAN

R. Jordan

AMMON

Jericho
Heshbon

Mt Nebo

DEAD SEA

MOAB

Gaza

NEGEB

WILDERNESS OF ZIN

Kadesh-barnea

Punon

ARABIAN DESERT

Makheloth

EDOM

WILDERNESS OF PARAN

Jotbathah
Ezion-geber

Hazeroth

MIDIAN

GULF OF AQABA

Inset map

Shiloh

R. Jordan

Bethel Ai

Gibeon Gilgal

Jericho Shittim

Jebus (Jerusalem) Beth-peor

Mt Nebo

DEAD SEA

MAP 5
Crossing Jordan

After forty years in the Wilderness, and after Moses had died, the Israelites crossed the river Jordan from Moab into the Promised Land.

View from Mount Nebo, where Moses died.

9

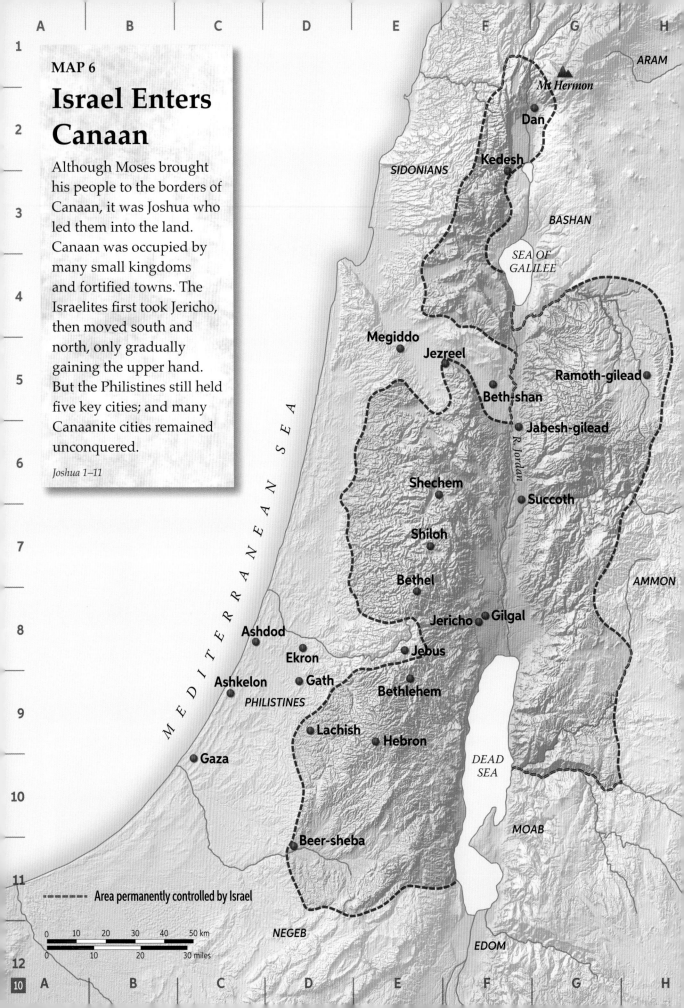

MAP 6

Israel Enters Canaan

Although Moses brought his people to the borders of Canaan, it was Joshua who led them into the land. Canaan was occupied by many small kingdoms and fortified towns. The Israelites first took Jericho, then moved south and north, only gradually gaining the upper hand. But the Philistines still held five key cities; and many Canaanite cities remained unconquered.

Joshua 1–11

ARAM

Mt Hermon

Dan

Kedesh

SIDONIANS

BASHAN

SEA OF GALILEE

Megiddo

Jezreel

Ramoth-gilead

Beth-shan

Jabesh-gilead

R. Jordan

Shechem

Succoth

Shiloh

Bethel

AMMON

Jericho   Gilgal

Ashdod

Jebus

Ekron

Ashkelon   Gath

Bethlehem

PHILISTINES

Lachish   Hebron

Gaza

DEAD SEA

M E D I T E R R A N E A N   S E A

MOAB

Beer-sheba

- - - - - Area permanently controlled by Israel

0   10   20   30   40   50 km
0   10   20   30 miles

NEGEB

EDOM

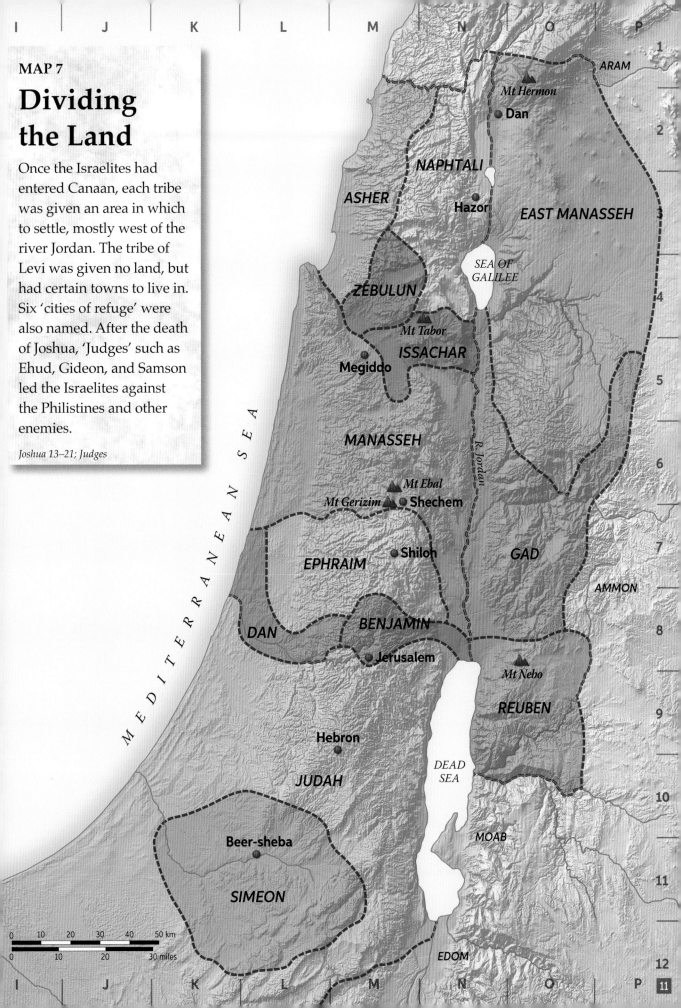

MAP 7

Dividing the Land

Once the Israelites had entered Canaan, each tribe was given an area in which to settle, mostly west of the river Jordan. The tribe of Levi was given no land, but had certain towns to live in. Six 'cities of refuge' were also named. After the death of Joshua, 'Judges' such as Ehud, Gideon, and Samson led the Israelites against the Philistines and other enemies.

Joshua 13–21; Judges

ARAM

Mt Hermon

● Dan

NAPHTALI

ASHER

Hazor

EAST MANASSEH

SEA OF GALILEE

ZEBULUN

Mt Tabor

ISSACHAR

Megiddo

M E D I T E R R A N E A N   S E A

MANASSEH

R. Jordan

Mt Ebal

Mt Gerizim ● Shechem

EPHRAIM

Shiloh

GAD

AMMON

DAN

BENJAMIN

Jerusalem

Mt Nebo

REUBEN

Hebron

DEAD SEA

JUDAH

Beer-sheba

MOAB

SIMEON

0 10 20 30 40 50 km
0 10 20 30 miles

EDOM

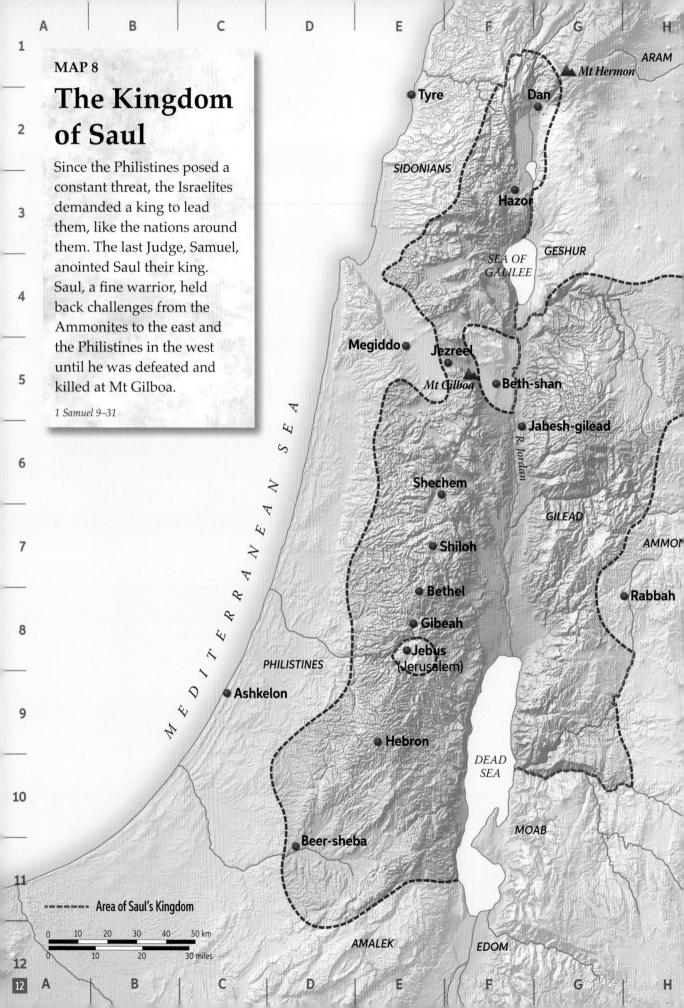

MAP 8

The Kingdom of Saul

Since the Philistines posed a
constant threat, the Israelites
demanded a king to lead
them, like the nations around
them. The last Judge, Samuel,
anointed Saul their king.
Saul, a fine warrior, held
back challenges from the
Ammonites to the east and
the Philistines in the west
until he was defeated and
killed at Mt Gilboa.

1 Samuel 9–31

- - - - Area of Saul's Kingdom

| 0 | 10 | 20 | 30 | 40 | 50 km |
| 0 | | 10 | 20 | | 30 miles |

ARAM

Mt Hermon

Tyre

Dan

SIDONIANS

Hazor

GESHUR

*SEA OF
GALILEE*

Megiddo

Jezreel

Mt Gilboa

Beth-shan

Jabesh-gilead

R. Jordan

Shechem

GILEAD

AMMON

Shiloh

Bethel

Rabbah

Gibeah

Jebus
(Jerusalem)

PHILISTINES

Ashkelon

Hebron

*DEAD
SEA*

Beer-sheba

MOAB

M E D I T E R R A N E A N   S E A

AMALEK

EDOM

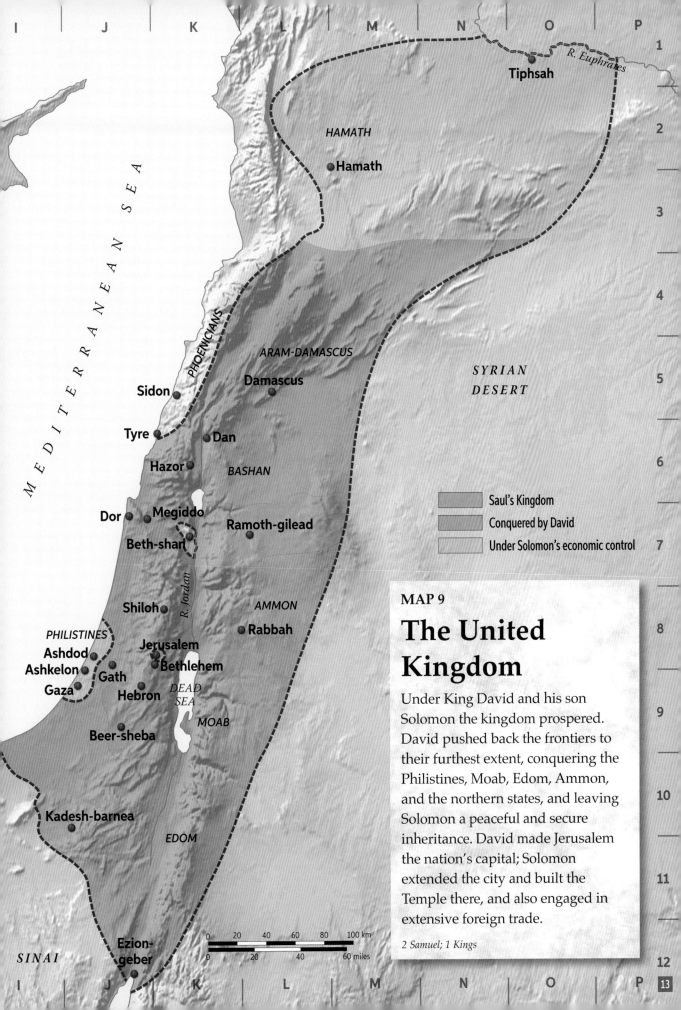

R. Euphrates

Tiphsah

HAMATH

Hamath

MEDITERRANEAN SEA

PHOENICIANS

ARAM-DAMASCUS

SYRIAN DESERT

Sidon

Damascus

Tyre

Dan

Hazor

BASHAN

Dor

Megiddo

Ramoth-gilead

Beth-shan

R. Jordan

Shiloh

AMMON

Rabbah

PHILISTINES

Jerusalem

Ashdod

Bethlehem

Ashkelon

Gath

Gaza

Hebron

DEAD SEA

Beer-sheba

MOAB

Kadesh-barnea

EDOM

SINAI

Ezion-geber

	Saul's Kingdom
	Conquered by David
	Under Solomon's economic control

0   20   40   60   80   100 km
0   20   40   60 miles

MAP 9

The United Kingdom

Under King David and his son Solomon the kingdom prospered. David pushed back the frontiers to their furthest extent, conquering the Philistines, Moab, Edom, Ammon, and the northern states, and leaving Solomon a peaceful and secure inheritance. David made Jerusalem the nation's capital; Solomon extended the city and built the Temple there, and also engaged in extensive foreign trade.

2 Samuel; 1 Kings

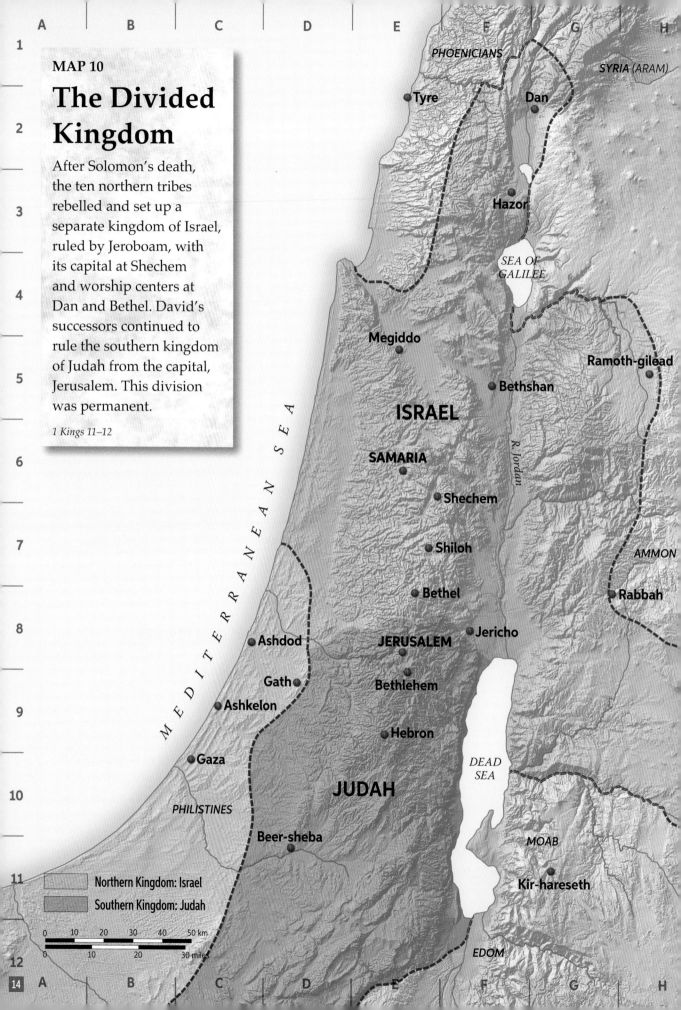

MAP 10
The Divided Kingdom

After Solomon's death, the ten northern tribes rebelled and set up a separate kingdom of Israel, ruled by Jeroboam, with its capital at Shechem and worship centers at Dan and Bethel. David's successors continued to rule the southern kingdom of Judah from the capital, Jerusalem. This division was permanent.

1 Kings 11–12

PHOENICIANS

SYRIA (ARAM)

Tyre

Dan

Hazor

SEA OF GALILEE

Megiddo

Ramoth-gilead

Bethshan

ISRAEL

R. Jordan

SAMARIA

Shechem

Shiloh

AMMON

Bethel

Rabbah

Ashdod

Jericho

JERUSALEM

Gath

Bethlehem

Ashkelon

Hebron

Gaza

DEAD SEA

JUDAH

PHILISTINES

Beer-sheba

MOAB

☐ Northern Kingdom: Israel

▨ Southern Kingdom: Judah

Kir-hareseth

MEDITERRANEAN SEA

EDOM

0 10 20 30 40 50 km
0 10 20 30 miles

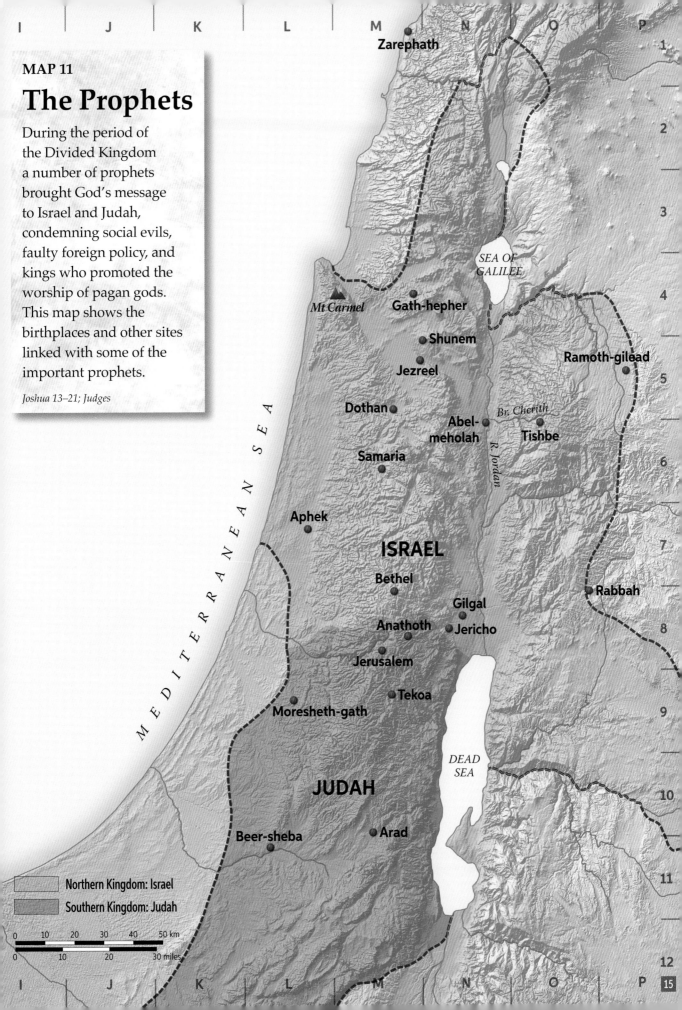

MAP 11

The Prophets

During the period of the Divided Kingdom a number of prophets brought God's message to Israel and Judah, condemning social evils, faulty foreign policy, and kings who promoted the worship of pagan gods. This map shows the birthplaces and other sites linked with some of the important prophets.

Joshua 13–21; Judges

Zarephath

SEA OF GALILEE

Mt Carmel

Gath-hepher

Shunem

Jezreel

Ramoth-gilead

Dothan

Br. Cherith

Abel-meholah

Tishbe

R. Jordan

Samaria

Aphek

ISRAEL

Bethel

Gilgal

Rabbah

Anathoth

Jericho

Jerusalem

Tekoa

Moresheth-gath

DEAD SEA

JUDAH

Beer-sheba

Arad

MEDITERRANEAN SEA

Northern Kingdom: Israel

Southern Kingdom: Judah

| 0 | 10 | 20 | 30 | 40 | 50 km |
| 0 | 10 | 20 | 30 miles |

FOUR EMPIRES

MAP 12

Assyria

about 650BC

The Assyrian Empire reached its peak of power between 880BC and 612BC. In 722BC Assyria destroyed the Northern Kingdom, Israel, deporting its people; and subdued Judah, the Southern Kingdom.

CASPIAN SEA

Carchemish
ASSYRIA
Nineveh
MEDIA
Asshur
R. Tigris
R. Euphrates
Damascus
ELAM
Babylon
Jerusalem
Susa
ARABIANS
Memphis
PER
R. Nile
EGYPT
PERSIAN GULF
RED SEA

0 100 200 300 400 500 km
0 100 200 300 miles

MAP 13

Babylon

about 550BC

The Babylonians took Nineveh, the Assyrian capital, in 612BC, and beat the Egyptians at Carchemish in 605BC. In 586BC Nebuchadn(r)ezzar destroyed Jerusalem and deported most of the people of Judah. So ended the Kingdom of Judah.

2 Kings 23–25

CASPIAN SEA

Carchemish
Nineveh
MEDIA
Riblah
R. Tigris
R. Euphrates
Ecbatana
SYRIA
Damascus
Babylon
Samaria
Jerusalem
Susa
BABYLONIA
Memphis
R. Nile
EGYPT
PERSIAN GULF
RED SEA

0 100 200 300 400 500 km
0 100 200 300 miles

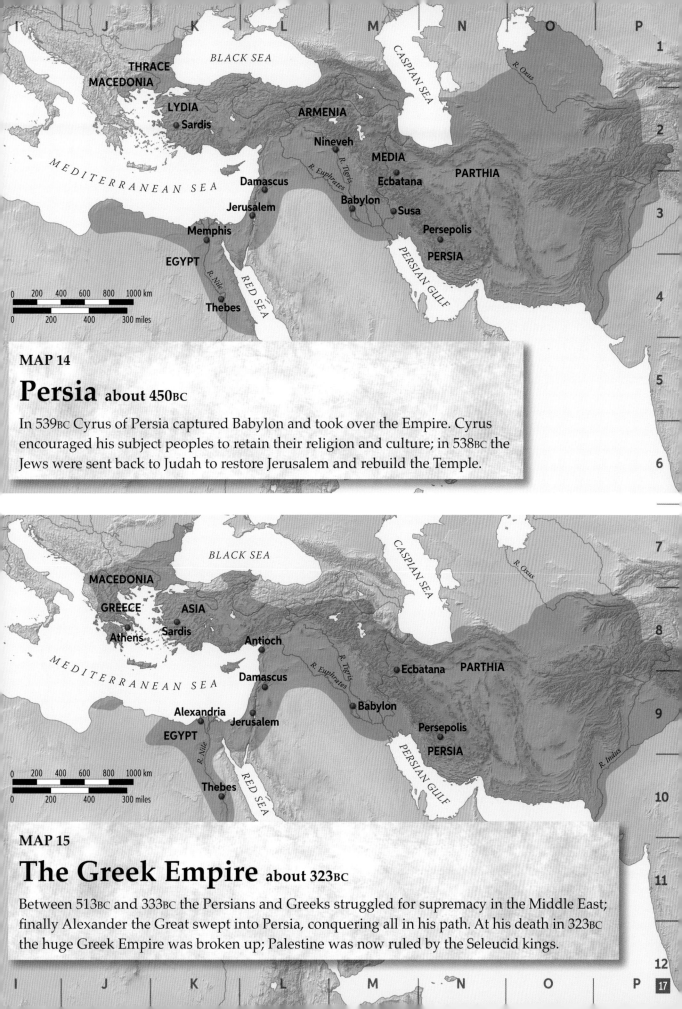

MAP 14

Persia about 450BC

In 539BC Cyrus of Persia captured Babylon and took over the Empire. Cyrus encouraged his subject peoples to retain their religion and culture; in 538BC the Jews were sent back to Judah to restore Jerusalem and rebuild the Temple.

MAP 15

The Greek Empire about 323BC

Between 513BC and 333BC the Persians and Greeks struggled for supremacy in the Middle East; finally Alexander the Great swept into Persia, conquering all in his path. At his death in 323BC the huge Greek Empire was broken up; Palestine was now ruled by the Seleucid kings.

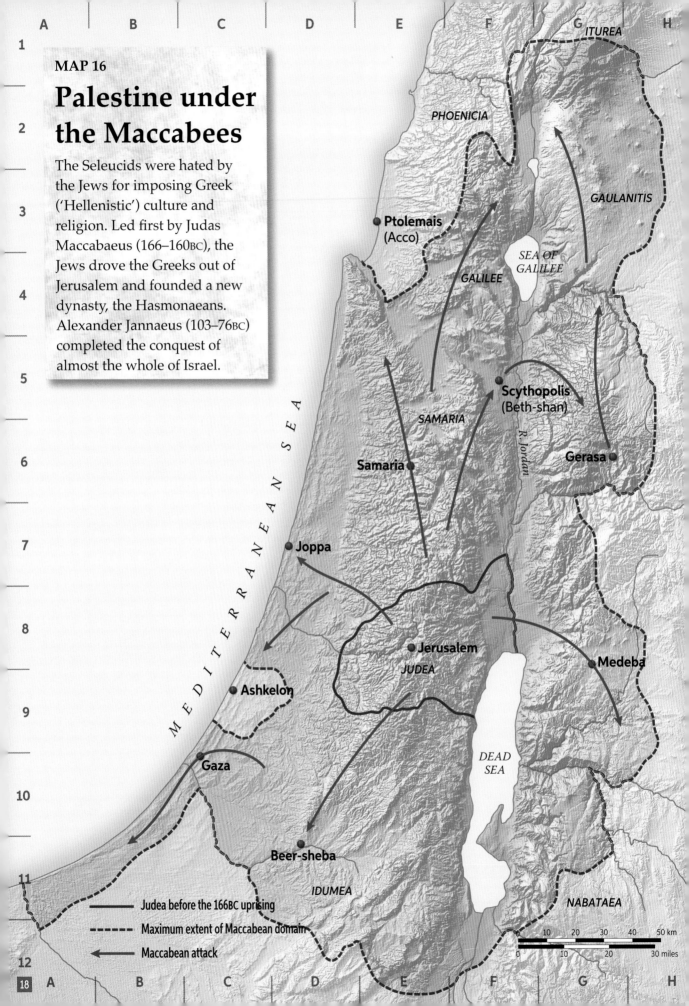

MAP 16

Palestine under the Maccabees

The Seleucids were hated by the Jews for imposing Greek ('Hellenistic') culture and religion. Led first by Judas Maccabaeus (166–160BC), the Jews drove the Greeks out of Jerusalem and founded a new dynasty, the Hasmonaeans. Alexander Jannaeus (103–76BC) completed the conquest of almost the whole of Israel.

ITUREA

PHOENICIA

● **Ptolemais**
(Acco)

*SEA OF
GALILEE*

GALILEE

GAULANITIS

SAMARIA

Scythopolis
(Beth-shan)

● **Samaria**

R. Jordan

Gerasa ●

● **Joppa**

● **Jerusalem**

JUDEA

● **Medeba**

● **Ashkelon**

*DEAD
SEA*

● **Gaza**

● **Beer-sheba**

IDUMEA

NABATAEA

M E D I T E R R A N E A N   S E A

— Judea before the 166BC uprising

--- Maximum extent of Maccabean domain

← Maccabean attack

| | 10 | 20 | 30 | 40 | 50 km |
| 0 | | 10 | | 20 | 30 miles |

MAP 17

Palestine Relief

The land of Palestine consists of a backbone of hill country, broken by the Plain of Megiddo, and bordered on the west by the coastal plain, and on the east by the deep Jordan Valley. East of the Jordan is a high plateau cut by four rivers. To the south lies the desert of the Negeb; to the north the mountains of Hermon and Lebanon. In the Jordan Valley, part of a deep rift valley stretching far into Africa, lies the Dead Sea, well below sea-level, and with no outlet.

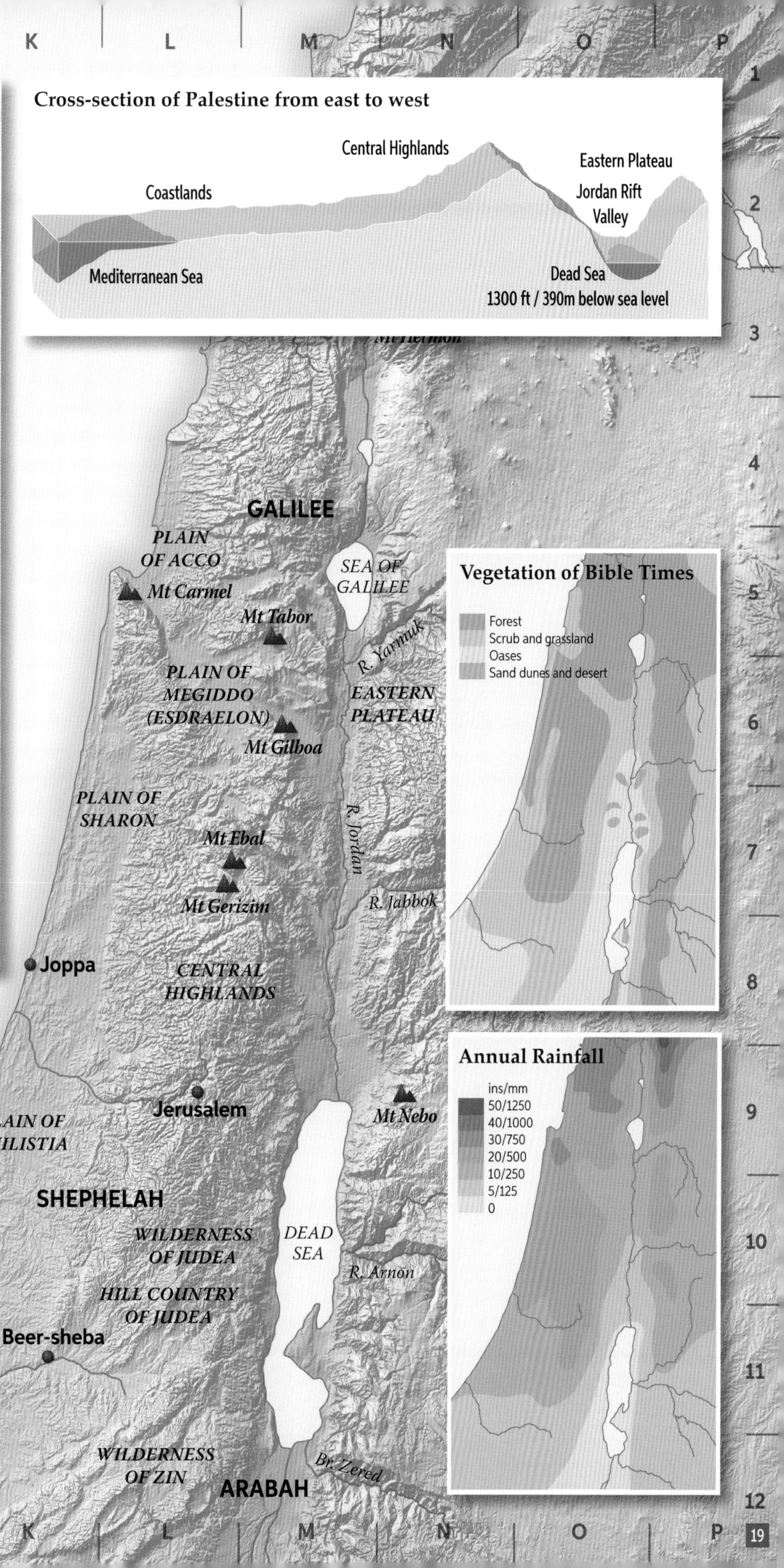

I J K L M N O P
1 2 3 4 5 6 7 8 9 10 11 12
Cross-section of Palestine from east to west
Central Highlands
Eastern Plateau
Coastlands
Jordan Rift Valley
Mediterranean Sea
Dead Sea
1300 ft / 390m below sea level
Mt Hermon
GALILEE
PLAIN OF ACCO
SEA OF GALILEE
Mt Carmel
Mt Tabor
R. Yarmuk
PLAIN OF MEGIDDO (ESDRAELON)
EASTERN PLATEAU
Mt Gilboa
PLAIN OF SHARON
R. Jordan
Mt Ebal
Mt Gerizim
R. Jabbok
Joppa
CENTRAL HIGHLANDS
MEDITERRANEAN SEA
Jerusalem
Mt Nebo
PLAIN OF PHILISTIA
SHEPHELAH
WILDERNESS OF JUDEA
DEAD SEA
R. Arnon
HILL COUNTRY OF JUDEA
Beer-sheba
WILDERNESS OF ZIN
Br. Zered
ARABAH
0 10 20 30 40 50 km
0 10 20 30 miles
Vegetation of Bible Times
Forest
Scrub and grassland
Oases
Sand dunes and desert
Annual Rainfall
ins/mm
50/1250
40/1000
30/750
20/500
10/250
5/125
0

A B C D E F G H

1
2
3

GAUL

R. Rhine

R. Danube

ITALY

Rome

4

SPAIN

5

Corduba

M E D I T E R R

SICILY

Syracuse

6

Carthage

AFRICA

7

MAURETANIA

8

MAP 18

The Roman Empire in the Time of Christ

By the first century AD the Romans had taken control of the Mediterranean area. The Romans soon began to unify their empire with roads, armies, and a vast public building programme, and with the Greek language and 'Hellenistic' culture.

9

10

11

12

A B C D E F G H

Ruins of the ancient forum, Rome.

I J K L M N O P

1

2

3

R. Danube

BLACK SEA

THRACE

4

MACEDONIA

Philippi

Byzantium

5

GREECE

ASIA

Pergamum

GALATIA

Corinth Athens

Ephesus

Tarsus

6

Antioch

R. Euphrates

7

N *E* *A* *N* *S* *E* *A*

CRETE

CYPRUS

SYRIA

Damascus

8

Tyre

Cyrene

Caesarea JUDEA

Jerusalem

CYRENAICA

Alexandria

9

Memphis

10

R. Nile

EGYPT

11

RED SEA

0 100 200 300 400 500 km

0 100 200 300 miles

12

I J K L M N O P

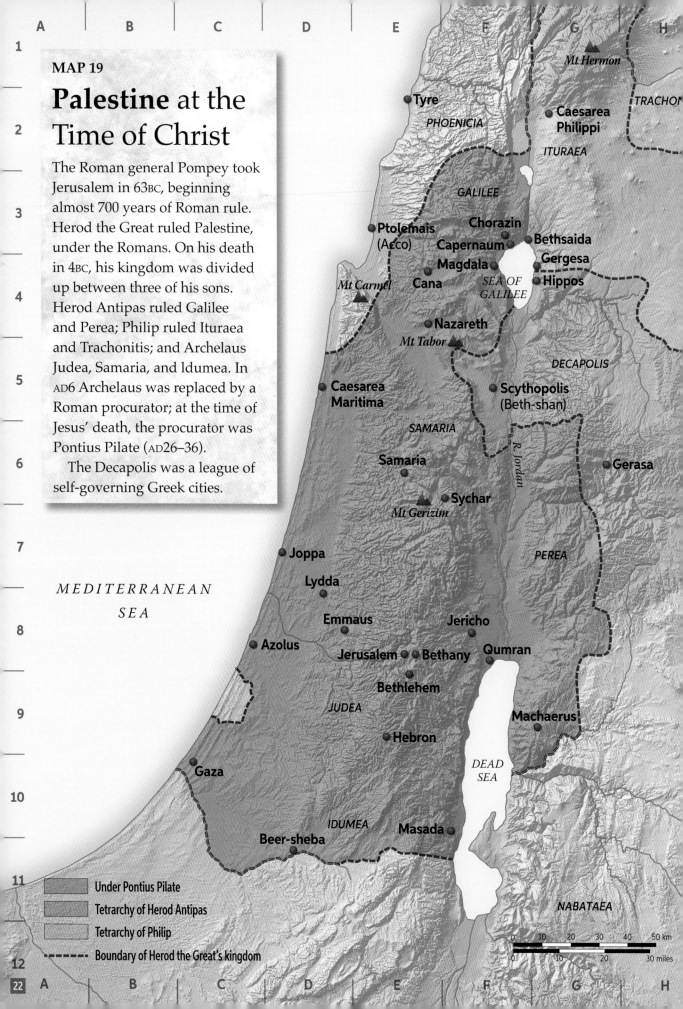

MAP 19

Palestine at the Time of Christ

The Roman general Pompey took Jerusalem in 63BC, beginning almost 700 years of Roman rule. Herod the Great ruled Palestine, under the Romans. On his death in 4BC, his kingdom was divided up between three of his sons. Herod Antipas ruled Galilee and Perea; Philip ruled Ituraea and Trachonitis; and Archelaus Judea, Samaria, and Idumea. In AD6 Archelaus was replaced by a Roman procurator; at the time of Jesus' death, the procurator was Pontius Pilate (AD26–36).

The Decapolis was a league of self-governing Greek cities.

Under Pontius Pilate
Tetrarchy of Herod Antipas
Tetrarchy of Philip
Boundary of Herod the Great's kingdom

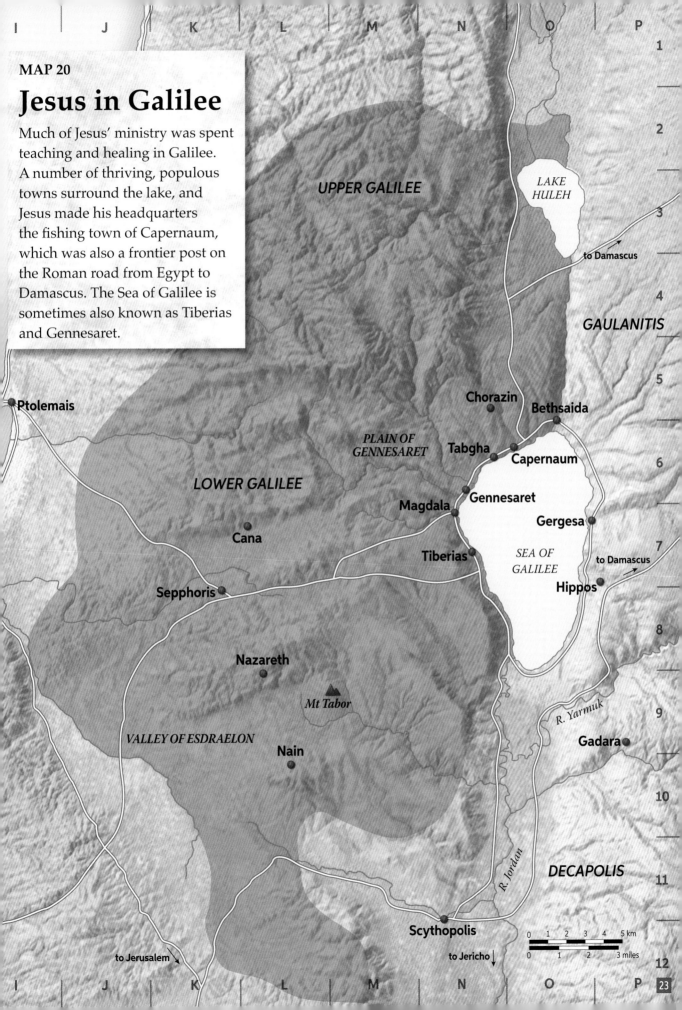

MAP 20

Jesus in Galilee

Much of Jesus' ministry was spent teaching and healing in Galilee. A number of thriving, populous towns surround the lake, and Jesus made his headquarters the fishing town of Capernaum, which was also a frontier post on the Roman road from Egypt to Damascus. The Sea of Galilee is sometimes also known as Tiberias and Gennesaret.

UPPER GALILEE

LAKE HULEH

to Damascus

GAULANITIS

Ptolemais

Chorazin

Bethsaida

PLAIN OF GENNESARET

Tabgha

Capernaum

LOWER GALILEE

Magdala

Gennesaret

Gergesa

Cana

Tiberias

SEA OF GALILEE

to Damascus

Sepphoris

Hippos

Nazareth

Mt Tabor

R. Yarmuk

VALLEY OF ESDRAELON

Gadara

Nain

R. Jordan

DECAPOLIS

Scythopolis

to Jerusalem

to Jericho

0 1 2 3 4 5 km

0 1 2 3 miles

MAP 21

Jerusalem at the Time of Christ

Herod the Great was a prodigious builder, and he made Jerusalem into a splendid city, crowned by the great Jewish Temple. Several Herodian remains have been discovered, including part of the steps to the Temple, as well as the Pools of Siloam and Bethesda. The map shows where the main events took place during Jesus' last days in Jerusalem.

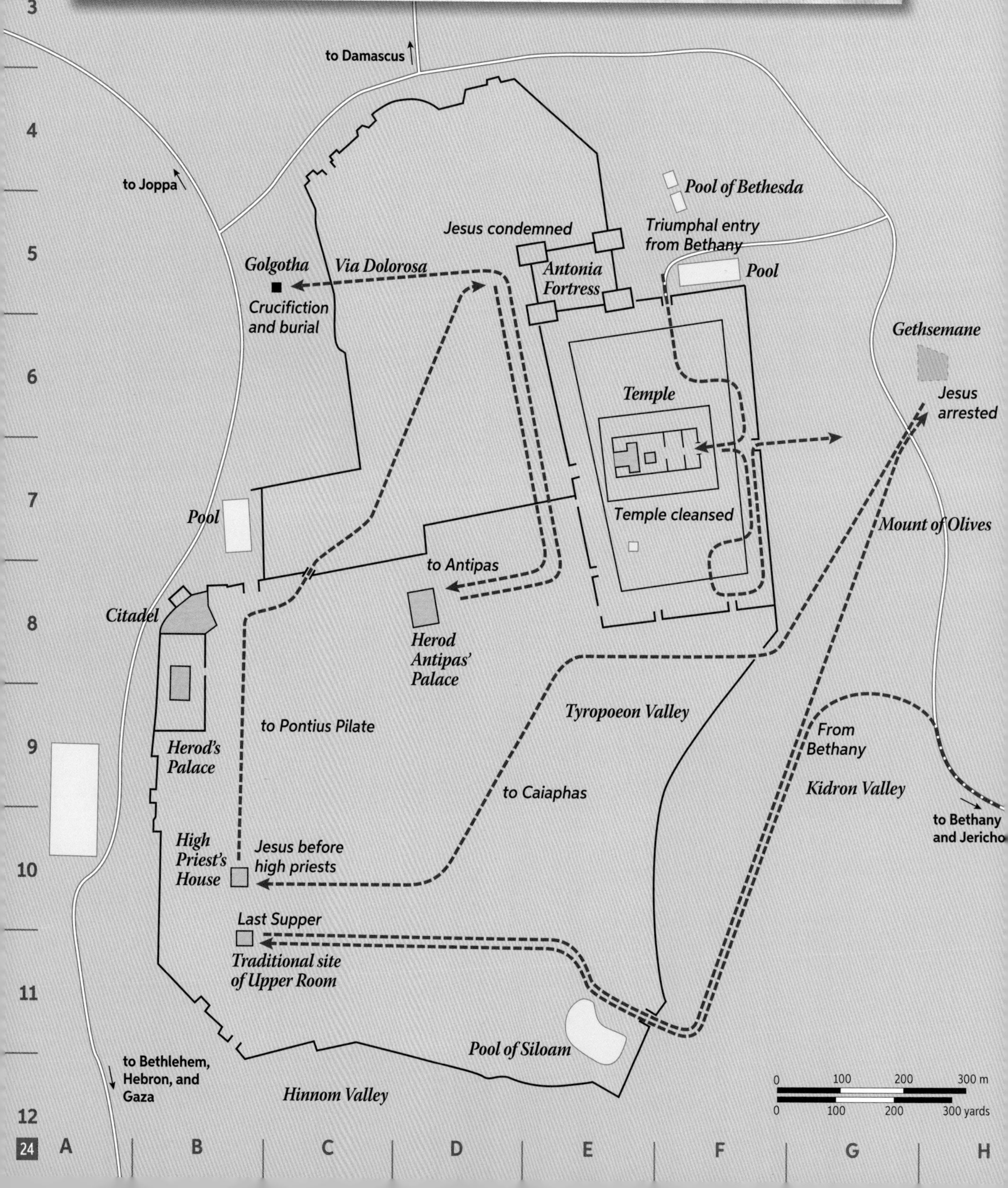

to Damascus

to Joppa

Pool of Bethesda

Jesus condemned

Triumphal entry from Bethany

Golgotha *Via Dolorosa* *Pool*

Antonia Fortress

Crucifiction and burial

Gethsemane

Temple

Jesus arrested

Temple cleansed

Pool

to Antipas

Mount of Olives

Citadel

Herod Antipas' Palace

to Pontius Pilate

Tyropoeon Valley

From Bethany

to Caiaphas

Kidron Valley

Herod's Palace

to Bethany and Jericho

High Priest's House Jesus before high priests

Last Supper

Traditional site of Upper Room

to Bethlehem, Hebron, and Gaza

Hinnom Valley

Pool of Siloam

0 100 200 300 m
0 100 200 300 yards

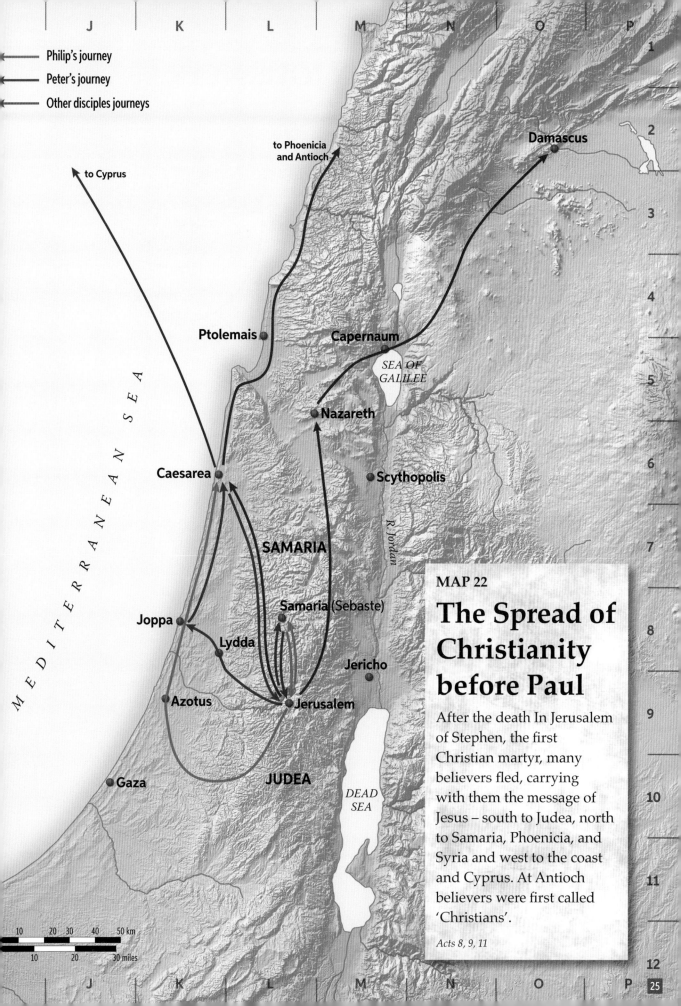

Philip's journey
Peter's journey
Other disciples journeys

to Cyprus

to Phoenicia
and Antioch

Damascus

Ptolemais

Capernaum

*SEA OF
GALILEE*

Nazareth

Caesarea

Scythopolis

M E D I T E R R A N E A N   S E A

R. Jordan

SAMARIA

Samaria (Sebaste)

Joppa

Lydda

Jericho

Azotus

Jerusalem

Gaza

JUDEA

*DEAD
SEA*

MAP 22

The Spread of Christianity before Paul

After the death In Jerusalem of Stephen, the first Christian martyr, many believers fled, carrying with them the message of Jesus – south to Judea, north to Samaria, Phoenicia, and Syria and west to the coast and Cyprus. At Antioch believers were first called 'Christians'.

Acts 8, 9, 11

10　20　30　40　50 km

10　20　30 miles

PAUL'S MISSIONARY JOURNEYS

MAP 23

First Journey

Paul set out on his first missionary journey in about AD47, accompanied by Barnabas and the young John Mark. John Mark left abruptly when they reached Perga. Paul and Barnabas arrived back in Antioch in AD49.

Acts 13–14

MAP 24

Second Journey

Accompanied by Silas, Paul left Antioch on his second journey in about AD50, and was joined by Timothy in Lystra, then by Luke in Troas. After 18 months in Corinth, Paul returned to Antioch in AD53.

Acts 15:36–18:22

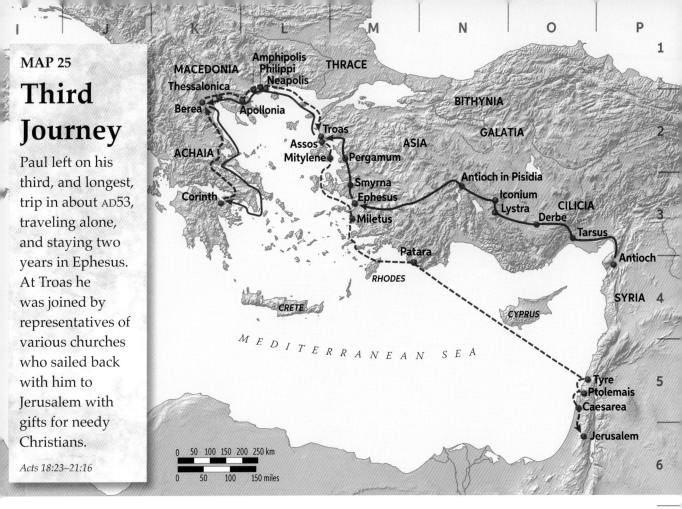

MAP 25

Third Journey

Paul left on his third, and longest, trip in about AD53, traveling alone, and staying two years in Ephesus. At Troas he was joined by representatives of various churches who sailed back with him to Jerusalem with gifts for needy Christians.

Acts 18:23–21:16

MACEDONIA
Thessalonica
Berea
Apollonia
Amphipolis
Philippi
Neapolis
THRACE
ACHAIA
Corinth
Troas
Assos
Mitylene
Pergamum
ASIA
Smyrna
Ephesus
Miletus
BITHYNIA
GALATIA
Antioch in Pisidia
Iconium
Lystra
Derbe
CILICIA
Tarsus
Antioch
Patara
RHODES
CRETE
CYPRUS
SYRIA
Tyre
Ptolemais
Caesarea
Jerusalem

MEDITERRANEAN SEA

0 50 100 150 200 250 km
0 50 100 150 miles

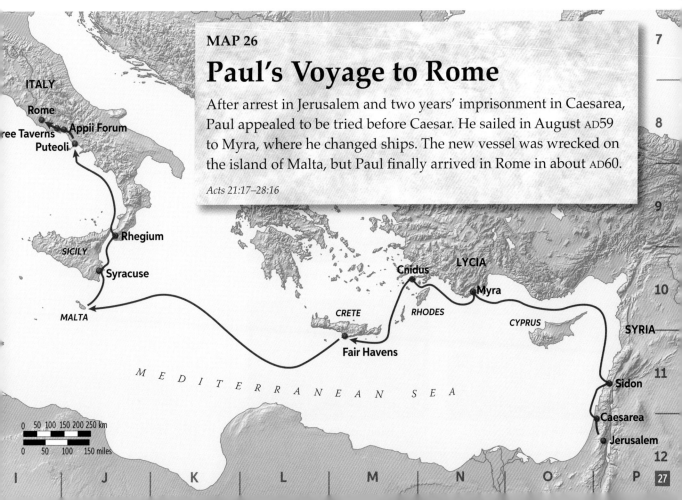

MAP 26

Paul's Voyage to Rome

After arrest in Jerusalem and two years' imprisonment in Caesarea, Paul appealed to be tried before Caesar. He sailed in August AD59 to Myra, where he changed ships. The new vessel was wrecked on the island of Malta, but Paul finally arrived in Rome in about AD60.

Acts 21:17–28:16

ITALY
Rome
ree Taverns
Appii Forum
Puteoli
Rhegium
SICILY
Syracuse
MALTA
Cnidus
LYCIA
Myra
CRETE
RHODES
CYPRUS
SYRIA
Fair Havens
Sidon
Caesarea
Jerusalem

MEDITERRANEAN SEA

0 50 100 150 200 250 km
0 50 100 150 miles

ITALY

† Rome

† Puteoli

MACEDONIA

Thessalonica †

† Berea

ACHAIA

Corinth † Ath

The Seven Churches of Asia Minor

Illustrated are the sites of four of the seven churches to which John addressed letters that we now find in the book of Revelation.

Ruins at Laodicea.

The forum, Smyrna (modern Izmir).

The theater, Pergamum.

The gymnasium, Sardis.

M E D I

† Cyrene

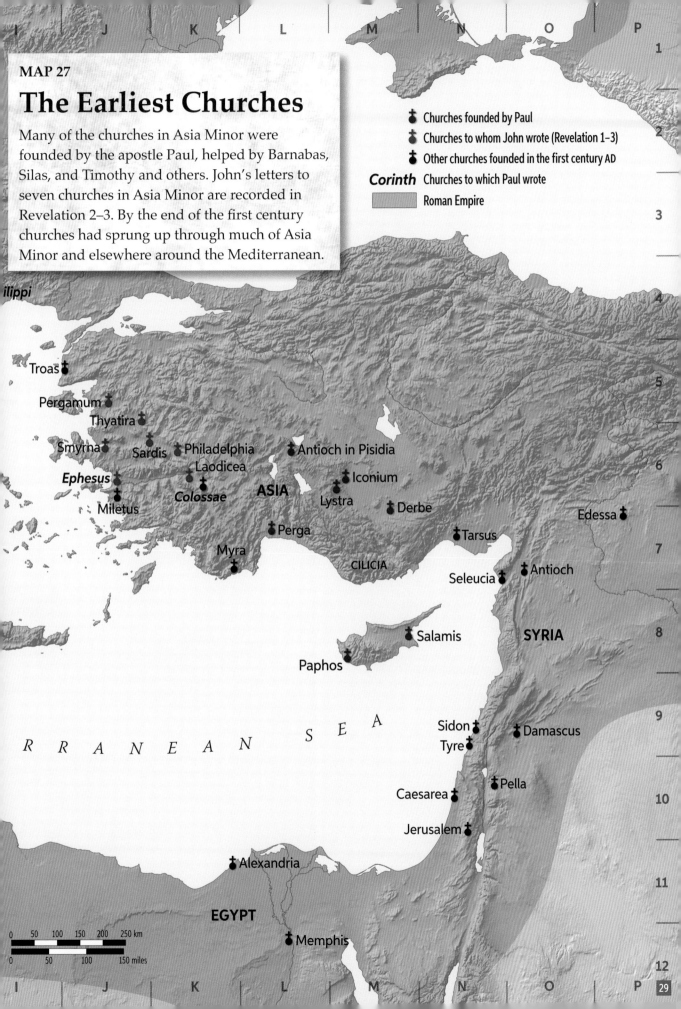

MAP 27

The Earliest Churches

Many of the churches in Asia Minor were founded by the apostle Paul, helped by Barnabas, Silas, and Timothy and others. John's letters to seven churches in Asia Minor are recorded in Revelation 2–3. By the end of the first century churches had sprung up through much of Asia Minor and elsewhere around the Mediterranean.

Churches founded by Paul
Churches to whom John wrote (Revelation 1–3)
Other churches founded in the first century AD
Corinth Churches to which Paul wrote
Roman Empire

ilippi

Troas

Pergamum
Thyatira
Smyrna
Sardis   Philadelphia
Laodicea   Antioch in Pisidia
Ephesus
   Colossae   Iconium
Miletus   ASIA   Lystra
         Derbe
      Perga   Tarsus
   Myra
      CILICIA   Edessa
            Seleucia   Antioch

         Salamis   SYRIA
Paphos

M E D I T E R R A N E A N   S E A

               Sidon   Damascus
               Tyre
                  Pella
            Caesarea
            Jerusalem

   Alexandria

EGYPT

0   50   100   150   200   250 km
0   50   100   150 miles

Memphis

29

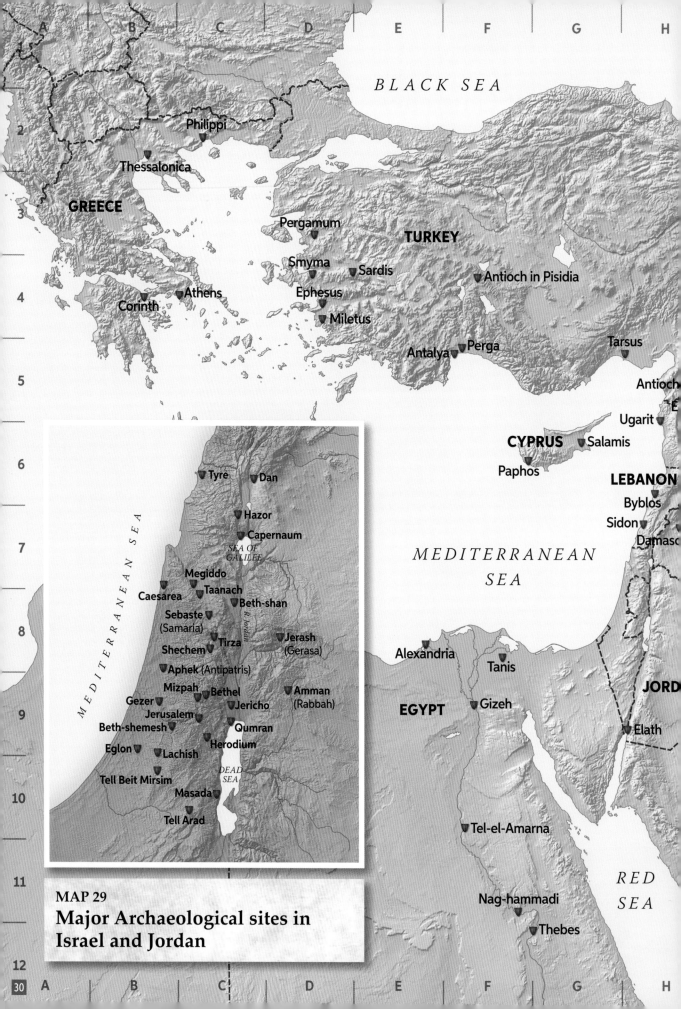

MAP 29
Major Archaeological sites in Israel and Jordan

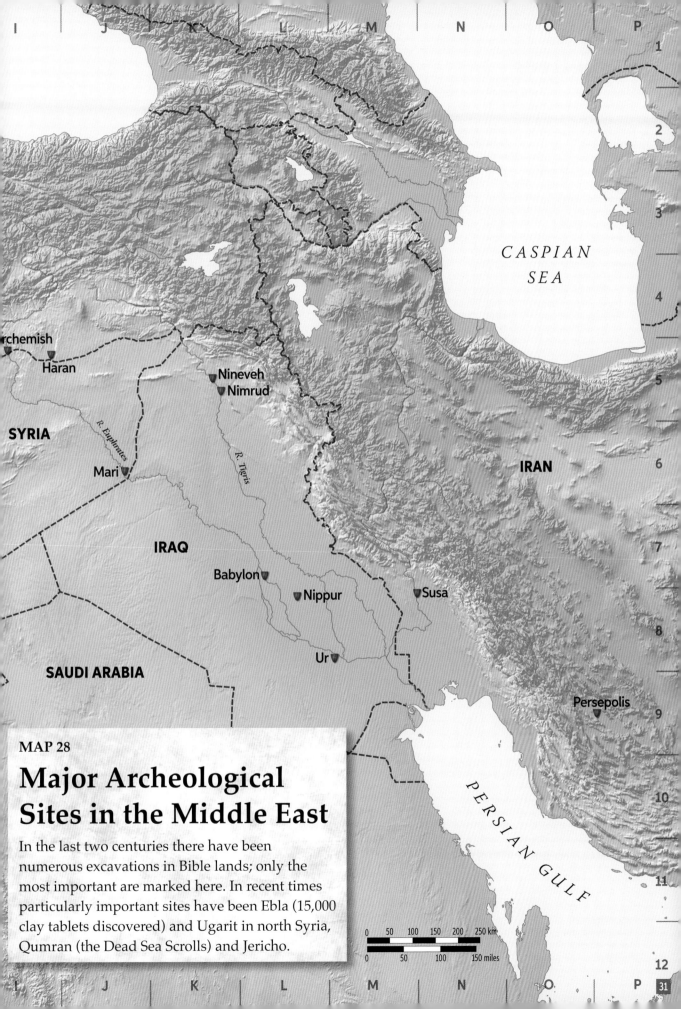

CASPIAN
SEA

rchemish

Haran

Nineveh
Nimrud

R. Euphrates

R. Tigris

SYRIA

Mari

IRAN

IRAQ

Babylon

Nippur

Susa

Ur

SAUDI ARABIA

Persepolis

PERSIAN GULF

MAP 28

Major Archeological Sites in the Middle East

In the last two centuries there have been numerous excavations in Bible lands; only the most important are marked here. In recent times particularly important sites have been Ebla (15,000 clay tablets discovered) and Ugarit in north Syria, Qumran (the Dead Sea Scrolls) and Jericho.

0 50 100 150 200 250 km

0 50 100 150 miles

Gazetteer

The first number refers to the Map number; the number and letter following to the grid reference.

Abel-meholah 11:5N
Achaia 24:8C; 26:2K
Acco, Plain of 17:5L
Alexandria 15:9K; 18:9M; 27: 11K; 28:8E
Aleppo 2 :5G
Amalek 8:12E
Ammon 4:3L; 6:8H; 7:8P; 8:7H; 9:8L; 10:7H
Amphipolis 24:8D; 25:1L
Anathoth 11:8M
Antalya 28:5F
Antioch 15:8L; 18:7O; 23:3H; 24:10H; 25:3P; 27:7O; 28:5H
Antioch in Pisidia 23:2E; 24:9F; 25:2N; 27:6L; 28:4F
Antipatris 29:8B
Aphek 12:7L; 29:8B
Apollonia 25:1L
Appii Forum 26:8I
Arad 10:10M
Aram 6:1H; 7:1P; 9:1H
Arnon, River 17:10M
Ashdod 6:9C; 9:8J; 10:8C
Asher 7:3M
Ashkelon 6:9C; 8:9C; 9:8J; 10: 9C; 16:9C
Asia 15:8K; 23:2E; 25:2N; 27:6L
Asshur 12:3F
Assos 25:2L
Assyria 3:4J; 13:2F
Attalla 23:3E
Athens 1:6E; 15:8J; 18:6K; 24:9D; 27:6H; 29:4C
Azolus 19:8C; 22:9K

Babylon 2:7L; 12:4F; 13:10F; 14:3M; 15:9M; 28:8L
Bashan 6:3G; 9:6L
Beersheba 3:6M; 6:11D; 7:11L; 8:11D; 9:11J; 10:11D; 11:11L; 16:11D; 17:11K; 20:11D
Benjamin 7:8M
Berea 24:8C; 25:1K; 27:5G
Bethany 19:8E
Bethel 3:3M; 6:8E; 8:8E; 10:8E; 11:7M; 29:9C
Bethesda 21:5F
Bethlehem 6:9E; 9:8K; 10:9E; 19:9E
Bethsaida 19:3E; 20:5O
Beth-shan 6:5F; 8:5F; 9:7K; 10:5F; 16:5F; 29:8C
Beth-shemesh 29:9B
Byblos 28:6H
Byzantium 18:5L

Caesarea (Maritima) 18:8N; 19:5D; 22:6K; 24:11G; 25:5O; 26:11P; 27:10N
Caesarea Philippi 19:2G
Cana 19:4E; 20:7L
Canaan 2:8F; 4:2J
Capernaum 19:3F; 20:6N; 22:5M; 29:7C

Carchemish 12:2E; 13:9E; 28:5I
Carmel, Mount 11:4L; 17:5L; 19:4E
Carthage 18:6G
Cenchreae 24:9C
Cherith, Brook 11:5N
Chorazin 19:3F; 20:5N
Cilicia 23:3G; 24:9G; 27:7M
Cnidus 26:10M
Colossae 27:6K
Corinth 18:6J; 24:9C; 25:2K; 27:6H; 28:4B
Crete 26:10M
Cyprus 23:4G
Cyrene 18:8J; 27:10G

Damascus 3: 1O; 9:5L; 12:3D; 13:10D; 14:3L; 15:9L; 18:8O; 27:9O; 28:7H
Dan 6:2F: 7:2N; 8:2F; 9:6K; 10:2F; 29:6C
Dan (tribe) 7:8L
Danube 18:2H
Dead Sea 10:10F; 22:10M
Decapolis 19:5G; 20:11O
Derbe 23:3F; 24:9G; 25:3O; 27:7M
Dor 9:7J
Dothan 3:3N; 11:5M

Ebal, Mount 7:6M; 17:7L
Ebla 28:5H
Ecbatana 13:9G; 14:2M; 15:8M
Edessa 27:7P
Edom 4:7K; 6:12F; 7:12N; 8:12F; 9:10K; 10:12F
Eglon 29:9B
Egypt 2:9D; 4:7C; 18:10M; 27:11K
Ekron 6:8D
Elam 12:4G
Elath 28:9H
Elim 4:9G
Emmaus 19:8D
Ephesus 18:6L; 24:9E; 25:2M; 27:6J; 28:4D
Ephraim 7:7L
Esdraelon, Valley of 20:9J
Euphrates, River 1:8K; 2:6J; 9:1O; 12:3F; 13:9F; 14:3L; 15:9L; 28:6J
Ezion-geber 4:9J; 9:12J

Fair Havens 26:10M
Fertile Crescent 1:7K

Gad 7:7O
Gadara 20:9P
Galatia 24:8F; 25:2N
Galilee 17:4M; 19:3F; 20
Galilee, Sea of 10:4F; 20:7O; 22:5M
Gath 6:9D; 9:8J; 10:9D
Gath-hepher 11:4M
Gaulantis 16:3G; 20:4O
Gaza 4:4I; 6:10C; 9:9J; 10:10C; 16:10C; 19:10C; 22:10J
Gennesaret 20:6N
Gerar 3:5M
Gerasa 16:6G; 19:6G; 29:8D

Gerizim, Mount 7:6M; 17:7L; 19:7E
Gergesa 19:4G; 20:7O
Geshur 8:4G
Gethsemane 21:6H
Gibeah 8:8E
Gilboa, Mount 8:5F; 17:6M
Gilead 8:7G
Gilgal 6:8F; 11:8N
Gizeh 28:9F
Golgotha 21:5C
Gomorrah 3:6N
Goshen 4:6E

Hamath 2:5G; 9:2M
Haran 2:4I; 28:5I
Hazeroth 4:10I
Hazor 3:2N; 7:3N; 8:3F; 9:6K; 10:3F; 29:7C
Hebron 2:8F; 3:5N; 6:9E; 7:9M; 8:9E; 9:9J; 10:9E; 19:9E
Heliopolis 2:9D
Hermon, Mount 6:1G; 7:1O; 8:1G; 19:1G
Heshbon 4:3L
Hippos 19:4G; 20:7O
Hittite Empire 2:4E
Huleh, Lake 20:3O

Iconium 23:2F; 24:9F; 25:2N; 27:6M
Idumea 16:11D; 19:10D
Issachar 7:5M
Iturea 16:1G; 19:2G

Jabbok, River 17:7M
Jabesh-gilead 6:6F; 8:6F
Jebus *see also Jerusalem* 6:8E
Jericho 4:3K; 6:8F; 10:8F; 11:8N; 19:8F; 22:8M; 29:9C
Jerusalem 7:8M; 8:8E; 9:8K; 10:8E; 11:8M; 12:4D; 13:10D; 14:3L; 15:9L; 16:8E; 17:9L; 18:9N; 19:8E; 21; 22:9L; 23:6G; 24:12G; 25:5O; 26:12P; 27:10N
Jezeel 6:5F; 8:5F; 11:5M
Joppa 16:7D; 17:8K; 19:7D; 22:8K
Jordan, River 20:11N; 22:7M
Jotbathah 4:8J
Judah 7:10L
Judea 19:9D; 22:10L
Judea, Wilderness of 17:10L

Kadesh-barnea 4:6I; 9:10J
Kedesh 6:2E
Kir-hareseth 10:11 G

Lachish 6:9D; 20:9B
Laodicea 27:6K
Lydda 19:8D; 22:8K
Lystra 23:3F; 24:9F; 25:3N; 27:6M

Macedonia 14:2J; 15:7J; 24:7C; 25:1K; 27:4G
Machaerus 19:9G
Magdala 19:4F; 20:7N
Mahanaim 3:4O
Makheloth 4:7I
Malta 26:10J
Manasseh 7:6M
Marah 4:9G
Mari 2:6J; 28:6J
Masada 19:10F; 29:10C

Medeba 16:8G
Media 12:3G; 13:9G; 14:2M
Megiddo 6:5E; 7:5M; 8:5E; 9:7K; 10:5E; 29:7C
Megiddo, Plain of 17:6L
Memphis 2:10d; 4:8D; 12:5C; 13:11C; 14:3K; 18:9M; 27:12L
Mesopotamia 2:5J
Midian 4:10J
Miletus 25:3M; 27:6J; 28:4D
Mitylene 25:2M
Mizpah 29:9C
Moab 4:4K; 6:10F; 7:10O; 8:10F; 9:9K; 10:11G
Moresheth-gath 11:9L
Myra 26:10N; 27:7K

Nabataea 16:11G; 19:11G
Nag-hammadi 28:11F
Nain 20:10L
Naphtali 7:2N
Nazareth 19:4E; 20:9L; 22:5L
Neapolis 24:7D; 25:1L
Nebo, Mount 4:3L; 7:8O; 17:9N
Negeb(v) 4:5J; 6:12D
Nimrud 28:5K
Nineveh 12:3F; 13:9F; 14:2M; 28:5K
Nippur 28:8L
Noph (Memphis) 2:10D; 4:8D

On (Heliopolis) 2:9D; 4:7D
Oxus, River 15:7O

Pamphylia 23:3F
Paphos 23:4F; 27:8M; 28:6F
Paran, Wilderness of 5:7I
Parthia 14:2N; 15:8N
Patara 25:3N
Pella 27:10N
Perea 19:7G
Perga 23:3E; 27:7L; 28:5F
Pergamum 19:5L; 25:2M; 27:5J; 28:3D
Persepolis 14:3N; 15:19M;28:9O
Persia 14:3N
Philadelphia 27:6K
Philippi 18:6K; 24:7D; 25:1L; 27:4I; 28:2C
Philistia, Plain of 17:9K
Philistines 6:9C; 8:8D; 9:8I
Phoenicia(ns) 9:5K; 10:1E; 16:2F; 19:2E
Phrygia 23:2E
Pisidia 23:2E
Pithom 4:6E
Ptolemais 16:3E; 19:3E; 20:5I; 22:4L; 25:5O
Punon 4:6K
Puteoli 26:8J; 27:4C

Qumran 19:8F; 29:9C

Rabbah 8:8H; 9:8L; 29:9D
Rameses (Zoan) 4:5E
Ramoth-gilead 6:5H; 9:7L; 10:5H; 11:5P
Red Sea 4: 10G
Reuben 7:9O
Rhegium 26:9J
Rhine, River 18:2F
Rhodes 25:3M; 26:10N
Riblah 13:9E

Rome 1:4A; 18:4H; 26:8I; 27:3C
Salamis 23:4G; 27:8M; 28:6G
Samaria 10:6E; 11:6M; 13:10D; 16:6E; 19:6E; 22:7L; 24:11G; 29:8C
Sardis 14:2K; 15:8K; 27:6J; 28:4D
Scythopolis 16:5F; 19:5F; 20:11N
Seleucia 23:4H; 27:7N
Sepphoris 20:7K
Sharon, Plain of 17:7K
Shechem 2:8F; 3:4N; 6:6E; 7:6M; 8:6E; 10:6E; 29:8C
Shephelah 17:10K
Shiloh 6:7E; 7:7M; 8:7E; 9:8K; 10:7E
Shunem 11:5M
Shur, Wilderness of 4:5F
Sidon(ians) 6:2E; 8:2E; 9:5K; 26:11P; 27:9N; 28:7H
Siloam, Pool of 21:11E
Simeon 7: 11L
Sinai, Mount 4:11H
Smyrna 25:2M; 27:6J; 28:4D
Sodom 3:6N
Succoth (Canaan) 3:4O;6:6F
Succoth (Egypt) 4:6F
Sumer 2:8L
Susa 12:4G; 13:10G; 14:3M; 28:8N
Sychar 19:6F
Syracuse 26:10J
Syria 10:1G; 23:4H; 25:4P; 27:8O

Taanach 29:8C
Tabgha 20:6N
Tabor, Mount 7:4N; 17:5M; 19:5F; 20:9M
Tanis 28:8F
Tarsus 18:6N; 23:3G; 24:9G; 25:3O; 27:7N; 28:5H
Tekoa 11:9M
Tel-ei-Amarna 28:10F
Thebes 14:4K; 15:10K; 28:12G
Thessalonica 24:8C; 25:1K; 27:4H; 28:2B
Thrace 14:1J; 24:7E; 25:1M
Three Taverns 26:8I
Thyatira 27:5J
Tiberias 20:7N
Tigris, River 2:6K; 12:3F; 13:9F; 14:3M; 15:8M; 28:6L
Tiphsah 9:1O
Tirza 29:8C
Tishbe 11:3N
Trachonitis 19:2H
Troas 24:8E; 25:2L; 27:5J
Tyre 8:2E; 9:6K; 10:2E; 18:8N; 19:2E; 25:5O; 27:9N; 29:6C

Ugarit 28:5H
Ur 1:9M; 2:9M; 28:8M

Yarmuk, River 16:6M–5N; 20:9O

Zarephath 11:1M
Zebulun 7:4M
Zered, Brook 17:12M
Zin, Wilderness of 4:6J; 17:12L
Zoan (Rameses) 2:9D; 4:5E
Zoar 3:6N

THE STUDENT BIBLE ATLAS Revised Edition

Text Copyright © 1989, 1996, 2015 Tim Dowley

Design and cartography by Bounford.com

Cover design: Alisha Lofgren

Worldwide coedition organized and produced by Lion Hudson, Oxford, OX2 8DR UK

Library of Congress Cataloging-in-Publication Data

Print ISBN: 978-1-5064-0010-5

eBook ISBN: 978-1-5064-0050-1